JUNIOR KROLL AND COMPANY

BY BETTY PARASKEVAS

ILLUSTRATED BY MICHAEL PARASKEVAS

HARCOURT BRACE & COMPANY

SAN DIEGO   NEW YORK   LONDON

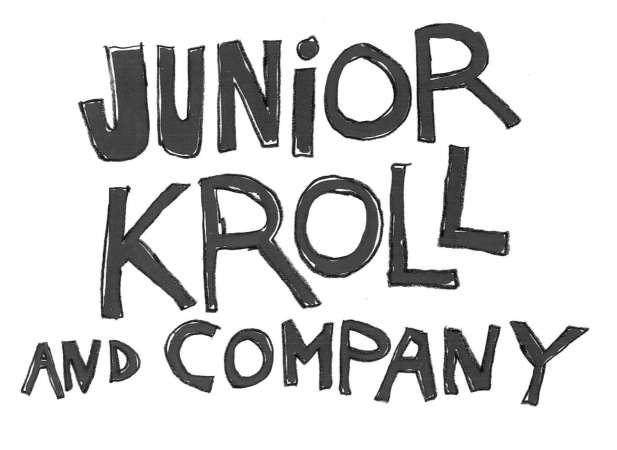

Text copyright © 1994 by Rita E. Paraskevas
Illustrations copyright © 1994 by Michael P. Paraskevas

Requests for permission to make copies of any
part of the work should be mailed to: Permissions
Department, Harcourt Brace & Company,
8th Floor, Orlando, Florida 32887.

Library of Congress Cataloging-in-Publication Data
Paraskevas, Betty.
Junior Kroll and company/by Betty Paraskevas;
illustrated by Michael Paraskevas.—1st ed.
p. cm.
Summary: Junior Kroll creates havoc in the family
with his saxophone lessons, pet parrot, and attempts
to get along with eccentric relatives.
ISBN 0-15-292855-3
1. Children's poetry, American.
[1. American poetry. 2. Humorous poetry.]
I. Paraskevas, Michael, 1961–   ill.
II. Title.
PS3566.A627J88 1994
811'.54—dc20   93-9138

PRINTED IN SINGAPORE

First edition
A B C D E

The illustrations in this book were done in gouache
on bristol board.
The display type was hand lettered by the illustrator.
The text type was set by Harcourt Brace & Company
Photocomposition Center, San Diego, California.
Color separations were made by Bright Arts, Ltd.,
Singapore.
Printed and bound by Tien Wah Press, Singapore
Production supervision by Warren Wallerstein and
Kent MacElwee
Designed by Michael Farmer

Junior Kroll has been a weekly feature in
Dan's Papers, Bridgehampton, New York,
since June 8, 1990.

And some things never change —
to Michael Farmer and Diane D'Andrade
—B.P. and M.P.

THE SAXOPHONE

Junior Kroll let it be known
He'd decided to master the saxophone.
Mrs. Kroll suggested piano, Mr. Kroll the violin.
But Junior persisted and in the end Mom and Dad gave in.
The brand new sax arrived along with Mr. Gold,
Who gave ten free lessons with each saxophone he sold.
Junior pressed the first valve down. Mr. Gold showed him how.
When he blew, what came out sounded like a cow.
For an hour this continued; Mr. Kroll quipped he could tell
Junior must have talent. That cow was beginning to smell.
Day twenty-seven and three lessons later Junior still gave it his all.
But it would take more than practice to get him to Carnegie Hall.
Junior pressed down the second valve. Grandfather chewed his cigar.
Mom wore her Walkman; Dad read *The Times* in his car.
Day thirty-four and Junior said
When he played the sax he got pains in his head.
For the sake of his health it was all too clear.
He must give up the sax! Poor little dear.
Then Junior said he wanted to paint, but he'd need a professional easel.
That's the way the money goes. Pop goes the weasel!

COUSIN HONEY DUFF

Junior Kroll's cousin, Honey Duff,
Came to stay with all her stuff.
In minutes Honey found a pair
Of high-heeled shoes and a hat to wear.
The part of Honey Duff between
The hat and the shoes could hardly be seen.
But monkey see, monkey do!
Whatever Junior did, Honey did, too.
Junior said, "Stop it, Honey!"
Honey said, "'top it, Honey!"
Junior Kroll stuck out his tongue,
Honey did, too, and landed among
The flowers on Mom's hibiscus plant.
"'uner push me," she began to chant.
Mrs. Kroll uprooted Honey's potted behind.
"She made me do it," Junior Kroll whined.
Tearfully eyeing each broken bloom
Mrs. Kroll said, "Junior! Go to your room!"
For three long days the war raged on.
Mrs. Kroll's patience was almost gone.
Then Aunt Jane returned for Honey Duff
In her little fur coat and her little fur muff.
They waited for Honey to say good-bye.
But instead,"Wanna stay," she began to cry.
"Oh, pleeeeease!" cried Junior. "Just one more day."
Mrs. Kroll watched Aunt Jane drive away.
And there was Junior trying to teach
His cousin Honey how to reach
The end of her nose with the tip of her tongue.
Poor Mrs. Kroll's nerves were nearly unstrung.
She wondered when her hibiscus would bloom.
Well, not before Junior went back to his room.

DANCING LESSON

Junior Kroll didn't like Blanche.
She was Grandfather's cousin and came from a branch
Of the family they all preferred to forget.
Yet there she sat with her long cigarette,
Boring everyone with her yak, yak, yak.
They called her the Merry Widow behind her back.
She said, "Come on, Junior, here's your chance.
Let's play some waltzes and I'll teach you to dance."
When the music began she was well past her prime,
But the years disappeared in three-quarter time.
"One, two, three. One, two, three,"
Sang the Merry Widow. "Follow me."
Junior struggled to follow along.
Blanche just kept dancing like nothing was wrong.
"Oh, beautiful stream, so clear and blue,
Don't look at your feet, for that's taboo."
He fell into step and they waltzed till Mom said
It was time for Junior to go to bed.

Blanche came in June and stayed through September.
Junior Kroll would always remember,
Whenever he heard "The Blue Danube" played,
That special summer and the friend he made.
She married her fifth, and this time Blanche
Found a man who owned a mahogany ranch,
Deep in Brazil. She wrote now and then,
But Junior never saw her again.
She sent him a gift I'll tell you about.
So turn the page if you'd like to find out.

THE GIFT

Junior Kroll tried to think
As he gazed in the mirror over the sink,
What it could be. This was the day.
Air Freight had called. It was on its way.
A present for Junior, she'd written ahead.
She hoped it would survive. That's all she said.
Mom and Dad weren't thrilled with that clue.
Crazy Max was a handful, but what could they do?
Junior practiced the art of surprise,
Dropping his jaw and stretching his eyes.
He'd keep his cool and say something clever,
Like, "This is too much! Well, I never
Expected anything as special as this.
I wish Blanche were here. I'd give her a kiss."

Just at that moment he heard Mother call,
"Junior, it's here," and he rushed to the hall.
Keeping his cool was forgotten when he saw
Through the slats of a crate a handsome macaw.
From the moment that bird saw Junior Kroll
It was fatal attraction, heart and soul.
"Wie Geht's!" he squawked. "My name is Arty.
I vas never a member of the Nazi Party."
Dad opened the crate and out Arty hopped.
Junior laughed and the Krolls' eyes popped.
When Junior asked, "What else can you say?"
Arty sang, "On the road to Mandalay!"

ARTY SETTLES IN

Junior Kroll's family didn't like that bird,
So they placed him in the sun room where he couldn't be heard.
He talked all day, and the things he said
Would boggle the mind and turn faces red.
He spoke Portuguese, English, and also German.
It was very difficult to determine
Just how long he'd been around,
But the vet assured them he was physically sound.
Mrs. Kroll suggested they send him back.
Dad proposed a trip down the river in a sack.
Grandfather lit his cigar and puffed,
Then suggested that Arty might be very nice stuffed.
Junior pleaded, "Arty, be still!"
Arty hopped up on the windowsill.
He saw Max in the yard and tapped on the pane.
Max looked in and they both went insane.
Every time Max barked, Arty barked too.
Poor little Junior didn't know what to do.
Jenny the maid saw Max jump at the window ledge.
She rushed outside to pull him away and fell in the privet hedge.
Junior got Arty back in his cage
Mrs. Kroll rushed in, red with rage.
"Watch your step, bird!" she cried.
Arty cocked his head and calmly replied,
   "If I should die, think only this of me,
      That there's some corner of a foreign field
      That is forever England!"
Junior saw her surprise and said, "Please, can't he stay?"
Mrs. Kroll murmured "That's Rupert Brooke…"
   and silently walked away.

JUNIOR KROLL AND PEAS

Junior Kroll said, "Excuse me, please."
Mrs. Kroll said, "Sit down and eat those peas."
Junior held his nose and slipped back into his chair.
Peas smelled. Peas were dumb. Peas ought'a be square.
He thought of rolling the peas that fall
Off everyone's fork into one big ball.
He'd push that ball and he'd never stop
Till he pushed it over a mountaintop.
Whoa! Look at it go!
Heading straight for the road below.
He conjured up some gruesome scene.
A truck skids on that gooky green.
It flips on its side dumping a load
Of nice fresh peas all over the road.
Junior's fantasy was interrupted
And his integrity sadly corrupted
When Mom brought in the Key Lime Pie.
Junior heaved a sorrowful sigh
And slipped the peas to Crazy Max
Under the table, begging for snacks.
Later Mrs. Kroll found the peas,
Tapping her foot she asked, "What are these?"
"They must have rolled off my fork," Junior said.
Crazy Max sniffed and turned his head,
As if to say with his nose in the air,
"Peas smell. Peas are dumb. Peas ought'a be square!"

THE EASTER RABBIT

Junior Kroll saved his money
To buy the family an Easter bunny.
He considered milk chocolate and bittersweet,
With solid ears and solid feet.
There were bunnies with baskets of jelly beans
And stylish bunnies wearing tinfoil jeans.
But he couldn't find a bunny just right.
So Junior decided that perhaps he might
Find a bunny of glass or papier-mâché
That would brighten up more than one holiday.
He found bunnies that talked when you pulled their strings
And wind-up bunnies that did crazy things.
But Junior still couldn't make up his mind,
Until the day he happened to find
A bunny on a shelf in an antique store.
This was the one he'd been searching for.
This bunny was thin, about eighteen inches high.
His fur was all gone and so was one eye.
He had very long legs, and Junior saw
Through the hole in one knee he was stuffed with straw.
The label in his coat read 1933.
He had survived somehow with dignity.
When the family gathered for Junior's surprise,
Mrs. Kroll said an allergy was bothering her eyes.
Grandfather Kroll had to clear his throat,
And Dad kept fussing with the pocket of his coat.
Junior's bunny had touched each heart,
And every year remained a part
Of the Easter season in the house of Kroll.
A gift from Junior. Bless his soul.

IS THERE A MOUSER IN THE HOUSE?

Junior Kroll found a cat,
Brought it home, and it promptly sat
On a white satin chair in the living room
And had to be chased with the kitchen broom.
Dad said to have a cat was absurd,
They had enough trouble with Max and the bird.
Poor Junior doted on that thankless cat,
Who by afternoon grew miraculously fat
On chicken livers and three bowls of cream,
A diet that raised its self-esteem.
It scorned all Junior's attempts to please.
At five o'clock Junior wheezed his first wheeze.
During dinner he began to droop.
His nose was running in his soup.
When he sneezed in his bowl Mrs. Kroll said,
"Come on, Junior, you're going to bed."
She called Dr. Sprowls, a friend for years.
He examined Junior and said, "It appears
Something has triggered an allergy.
We must figure out what it might be."
Junior replied, "Excuse me, please.
I believe I might be allergic to peas!"
At that very moment in walked the cat.
Dr. Sprowls shook his head and that was that.
The cat, of course, came to no harm.
Dr. Sprowls took him off to a friend with a farm.
He gave Junior something to ease the attack,
And that thankless cat never looked back.

ARTY FALLS

Junior Kroll said, "Stop that, please."
But that macaw just loved to tease
Crazy Max. When Max took a snooze,
Arty did his best to blow Max's fuse.
He'd march up and down until he saw
Max just about to raise a paw.
Then he'd take off to a spot well protected,
Until one fateful day Max connected.
Arty fell with one terrifying shriek.
That devilish macaw had cracked his beak.
They called the vet who said their only hope
Was to press the beak in a soft cake of soap.
It would serve as a splint till they could get him there.
Mrs. Kroll felt faint and collapsed in a chair.
Junior said, "Excuse me, please.
Put your head between your knees.
I have to get a cake of soap."
Jenny the maid couldn't cope.
Flapping her apron she was out of control.
The burden fell on poor Junior Kroll.
He gently pressed Arty's beak
Into the soap—Arty was weak.
Max kept whimpering as he paced up and down.
Jenny the maid managed to drive them to town.
They were told they would have to leave Arty there,
And he was immediately placed in intensive care.
As Junior was getting ready for bed,
He noticed Max trembling and Junior said,
"Don't worry, Max. He'll be all right."
It took them both a long time to get to sleep that night.

WELCOME HOME, ARTY

Arty came home with his mended beak
And a clean bill of health, but he wouldn't speak.
Before he'd collided with Max's paw
None of them had liked that noisy macaw.
Now they gathered around that bird,
Pleading for just one single word.
Jenny the maid sang "Brazil," hoping the bird would join in.
Mom decided on Kipling with a verse from "Gunga Din."
Dad was less creative and said, "How's the beak?"
If he said it once he said it fifty times, but Arty wouldn't speak.
Grandfather Kroll was the most absurd.
He marched around that silent bird,
Chanting, "*Eins, zwei, drei, vier,*
We're all happy Arty's here."
One week went by, and each tried several times a day
To chat with the bird, but in a word, Arty had nothing to say.
Then one evening at dinner from the sun room came a sound,
And a quote they'd never heard before as Arty began to expound.
  "It matters not how strait the gate,
    How charged with punishment the scroll;
    I am the master of my fate,
    I am the captain of my soul!"
Crazy Max growled, and Mrs. Kroll got up and closed the door.
"Henley," she said shaking her head. "I never heard that one before."
Yes, Arty's reign was over. It lasted but a week.
Junior snickered and passed the peas. "He should have shut his beak!"

THE BASS FIDDLE

Junior Kroll saw an old bass fiddle
In a secondhand store, standing in the middle
Of a dingy window in between
A broken-down upright and a red velveteen
Camelback sofa. Junior opened the door
And picked a path across the cluttered floor.
"Excuse me, please. What's the price
Of that old bass fiddle?" He had to say it twice.
The old man turned, puffing his cigar.
"Four hundred big ones. How 'bout a nice cheap guitar?"
Waving away a cloud of smoke,
Junior coughed before he spoke.
"I'll give you three with one dollar down."
"There ain't a finer fiddle in town."
A wall of clocks ticked time away,
"Okay, gimme the dollar. You got three days to pay."
Now Junior Kroll was deep in thought.
How could he pay for what he'd bought?
He had the money in the bank, but that wouldn't do.
He couldn't get it without you know who.
Where does a kid go when he needs a loan
For something he wants to buy on his own?

Grandfather Kroll came through with the cash,
And Junior Kroll took off in a flash.
Back at the shop the old man put the bass
Into its shabby canvas case.
With two little wheels to make it roll,
And away went the fiddle and Junior Kroll.
You could hear folks laughing up and down the street.
All they saw was that fiddle on two little feet,
Bumping along, and the fiddle would say,
"Excuse me, please," as it hurried away.

Junior's bass fiddle was home at last.
Mrs. Kroll just stood there quite aghast.
"I bought it," Junior said, beaming with pride,
"Because it makes me feel good inside."
Mrs. Kroll just stared; she couldn't speak.
But leave it to that macaw to open his beak.
"A thing of beauty is a joy forever!"
Mrs. Kroll shook her head and said, "Well! I never!"

BUZZ, BUZZ, BUZZ

Junior Kroll tossed about.
He covered his head but his feet stuck out.
Better find out if the coast is clear.
So he carefully uncovered one little ear.
Oh, no! There it was,
'round and 'round, that relentless buzz.
It was on his foot. He sat up in bed,
Turned on the light. It was a piece of thread.
He rolled up his *Archie* comic book
And stood on the bed for a better look.
This is war. Check each wall.
Whoa, steady now. Don't want to fall.
"What's going on?" It was the voice of doom.
"There's a mutant mosquito in my room."

"Get back in that bed!"
"Oh, please, it's gonna bite."
"You heard what I said and turn off that light."
"In a minute." He stepped from the bed to the chair.
"Okay, skeeter, say a prayer!"
Wham! *Archie* hit the wall.
The mosquito escaped into the hall.
Junior jumped from the chair to the floor,
Rushed over and slammed the door.
"What was that? Are you all right?"
"I just closed the door and turned off the light."
Junior hummed a little tune and grinned a little grin.
He got that nasty skeeter out, and it couldn't get back in.
Mrs. Kroll tossed about,
Her head was covered but her feet stuck out.
It was on her foot! She snapped on the light.
A piece of thread? No! A mosquito bite.

FUZZY LiTTLE CHRISTMAS TREE

Junior Kroll was as busy as a bee
Making a little fuzzy Christmas tree
With bright green pipe cleaners. When the branches were done
He glued a red berry on the end of each one.
Then he placed the fuzzy little tree underneath his bed.
On Christmas Eve, in the afternoon, he put on his coat and said
He was going to visit the lady who lived at the end of the lane,
On a huge estate where the entrance was blocked by an iron chain.
He was holding his little fuzzy Christmas tree,
Now much fuzzier than it used to be,
When the butler escorted him to where
The old lady rested in her tapestried chair.
The tree was a work of art she declared,
And they chatted away while the butler prepared
A pot of hot tea and gingerbread squares;
And Junior tested each one of the chairs.
He had finished his third piece of gingerbread
When the old lady pointed to a box and said,
"Those books were mine. Now I'm giving them to you.
I shall have them delivered, but you may take a few."
Junior opened the box. "You bet I will!"
He took *The Bobbsey Twins on Blueberry Hill.*
The butler escorted Junior to the door and returned to see
The old lady in her tapestried chair smiling at Junior's tree.
"Edward," she said, "I'd like to extend
An invitation for dinner to a trusted friend."
"I'd be delighted, Madam," Edward said.
And long after Junior was tucked into bed,
They raised their steaming hot cups of tea
And toasted the fuzzy little Christmas tree,
And the boy who made it. Bless his soul.
"A very Merry Christmas to you, Junior Kroll!"